BIGHORN SHEEP

LIVING WILD

LIVING WILD

Published by Creative Education and Creative Paperbacks
P.O. Box 227, Mankato, Minnesota 56002
Creative Education and Creative Paperbacks are imprints of The Creative Company
www.thecreativecompany.us

Design and production by Mary Herrmann
Art direction by Rita Marshall
Printed in the United States of America

Photographs by Alamy (georgesanker.com, John E Marriott, Robert McGouey/
Wildlife, National Geographic Image Collection), Corbis (Sumio Harada/Minden
Pictures, Julie Jacobson/AP, Donald M. Jones/Minden Pictures), Creative Commons
Wikimedia (Andrew Barna, California Department of Fish and Wildlife, Dallas
Museum of Art, Robert N. Dennis collection of stereoscopic views, Joseph Smit, Ryan
Stavely, Rennett Stowe), iStockphoto (ChrisMR, gacooksey), Shutterstock (alexsvirid,
Brandon Alms, Wesley Aston, Nancy Bauer, Fribus Ekaterina, gnohz, Ronnie Howard,
jakit17, Jearu, Sarah Jessup, Vladimir Korostyshevskiy, Legacy Images, Mayskyphoto,
John McLaird, Mighty Sequoia Studio, David Osborn, James Marvin Phelps, Olga
Popova, Scott E Read, Tom Reichner)

Library of Congress Cataloging-in-Publication Data
Gish, Melissa.
Bighorn sheep / Melissa Gish.
p. cm. — (Living wild)
Includes bibliographical references and index.
Summary: A look at bighorn sheep, including their habitats, physical characteristics such
as their horns, behaviors, relationships with humans, and their endangered status in the
world today.
ISBN 978-1-60818-564-1 (hardcover)
ISBN 978-1-62832-165-4 (pbk)
1. Bighorn sheep—Juvenile literature. 2. Rare mammals—Juvenile literature. I. Title.

QL737.U53G565 2015
599.649'7—dc23   2014028003

CCSS: RI.5.1, 2, 3, 8; RST.6-8.1, 2, 5, 6, 8; RH.6-8.3, 4, 5, 6, 7, 8

HC 9 8 7 6 5 4 3 2
PBK 9 8 7 6 5 4 3 2 1

CREATIVE EDUCATION • CREATIVE PAPERBACKS

BIGHORN SHEEP

Melissa Gish

It is November in Colorado's Never Summer Wilderness, where two male bighorn sheep,

each weighing more than 250 pounds
(113 kg), are about to engage in battle.

It is November in Colorado's Never Summer Wilderness, where 600-year-old spruce and fir trees tower above snow-covered rocks and icy streams. Two male bighorn sheep, each weighing more than 250 pounds (113 kg), are about to engage in battle. They taunt each other with their front hooves and then raise themselves onto their hind legs. They run several steps toward each other. Then they freeze in midair for a split second before ramming their 30-pound (13.6 kg) curled horns into each other. Double-thick skulls absorb the shock of impact. Then the sheep back up, eye each other, and brace for another collision. A dozen other males look on, preparing to challenge the winner of this match. It is the time of year when the strongest males compete for the chance to mate. The one left standing will be the victor—the king of the mountain.

WHERE IN THE WORLD THEY LIVE

Rocky Mountain Bighorn Sheep
northern Canada to New Mexico

Sierra Nevada Bighorn Sheep
California

Desert Bighorn Sheep
northern Mexico and western United States

The seven subspecies of bighorn sheep are broadly classified as either "mountain" or "desert," according to their respective homes. The Rocky Mountain and Sierra Nevada subspecies live on or near North American mountain ranges, while five desert subspecies (California, Mexicana, Nelson's, Peninsular, and Weem's) are found in that dry habitat throughout the western United States and Mexico. The colored squares represent the general areas in which bighorn sheep are found today.

The bighorn sheep is the state animal of Colorado and the provincial animal of Alberta, Canada.

Bighorn sheep once roamed the western half of North America. Today, they are limited to parts of the Rocky and Sierra Nevada mountains and scattered throughout the high deserts of the southwestern United States and northern Mexico. The bighorn sheep is 1 of about 140 cloven-hoofed, hollow-horned members of the Bovidae family. It belongs to the genus *Ovis*, along with the rest of the world's sheep species. The largest wild sheep, the argali of Central Asia's Himalaya and Altai mountain ranges, is only slightly heavier than the bighorn sheep. Mouflon sheep of the Caucasus Mountains are believed to be the oldest sheep species and the ancestors of all living sheep. Northern Russia's snow sheep, sometimes called Siberian bighorn sheep, are more closely related to North American bighorn sheep than to their neighbors in Europe and Asia. The Dall sheep is the only other wild sheep species native to North America. Dalls live in the mountains of northwestern Canada and Alaska. Much smaller than their wild cousins, more than 200 breeds of **domesticated** sheep exist around the world.

Mimbres pottery from New Mexico featured geometric patterns and animals of the region, such as desert bighorns.

Scientists classify bighorn sheep based on their primary habitat—mountain or desert. Rocky Mountain bighorns are the most numerous of the mountain group, as 35,000 are found from New Mexico to British Columbia. A subspecies of mountain bighorn, the Audubon's bighorn, once ranged from Montana and Wyoming throughout the Dakotas, but by 1925, it had been hunted to **extinction**. Desert bighorns include 5 subspecies: About 13,000 Nelson's bighorns live in Utah, Arizona, Nevada, and California. Roughly 10,500 California bighorns can be found from North Dakota to Nevada, California, and British Columbia. Mexicana bighorns range from Arizona to Texas and Mexico. Only about 6,000 of this subspecies remain, and they are considered endangered in the state of New Mexico. About 2,500 Peninsular bighorns live in the northern part of Baja California, Mexico, while nearly 950 live in southern California, where they have been endangered since 1998. Fewer than 1,000 Weem's bighorns are found in the far southern part of Baja California. The International Union for Conservation of Nature (IUCN) lists the Weem's bighorn as a critically endangered species.

When their characteristic white rump is out of sight, desert bighorns can stay well hidden among the rocky landscape.

Bighorns in the lower Rocky Mountains typically begin shedding in June, while those in colder climates begin in July.

Bighorns and their relatives are mammals. All mammals, with the exceptions of the platypus and echidna, give birth to live offspring and produce milk to feed their young. Mammals are warm-blooded animals. This means that their bodies work to maintain a healthy temperature. Bighorns have a smooth coat of insulating fur that helps keep them warm in their high-altitude habitats. Darker fur around their neck is longer and coarser, offering added protection. The bighorn's coat, called pelage, varies from dark brown to grayish-brown in color with white patches on the muzzle, belly, and rump. In winter, bighorns grow a thicker coat, with the fur around their neck and chest growing shaggier. In spring, the sheep rub themselves on trees and rocks to loosen the fur and shed these winter coats.

Bighorn sheep are named for their impressive horns. Unlike the antlers of deer and moose, which are shed seasonally, horns never fall off unless they are broken off. The horns are made of bone covered with a layer of keratin—the same substance that is found in human fingernails. There is an air pocket between the bone and the keratin, which is why bovids are known as hollow-horned animals. Both males (called rams) and females (called ewes) have horns. Rams' horns are larger than those of ewes. Desert bighorns have smaller, less tightly curled horns than mountain bighorns. A mature mountain ram's horns can measure up to 30 inches (76.2 cm) in length and up to 15 inches (38.1 cm) around at the base. A set of horns can weigh as much as 30 pounds (13.6 kg) —more than the combined weight of all the bones in a bighorn's body. It takes seven to eight years for a male's horns to grow into a complete curl. Females' horns never grow beyond a half curl.

Barbary sheep, goat-antelopes native to North Africa, have been introduced to bighorn habitat in Texas, New Mexico, and California.

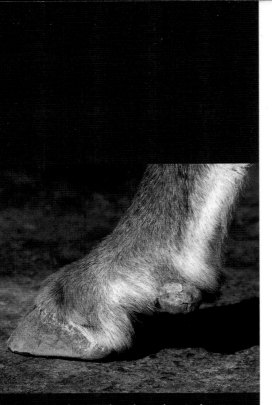

A sheep's dewclaws, located behind and above the hoof, helped prehistoric sheep walk but serve no purpose today.

Bighorn sheep can jump 20 feet (6.1 m) from one rock ledge to another and balance on ledges just 2 inches (5.1 cm) wide.

Like all bovids, males are typically larger than females. Bighorns rarely exceed heights of 3.5 feet (1.1 m) at the shoulder and lengths of 6.5 feet (2 m) from chest to tail. Male mountain bighorns can weigh up to 300 pounds (136 kg), but desert bighorns are slenderer, seldom weighing more than 250 pounds (113 kg). Females typically weigh about 100 pounds (45.4 kg) less than males. In general, bighorns' weight fluctuates with the seasons, as the animals add bulk in summer when food is plentiful and lose weight in winter when food is scarce. Despite their size, bighorn sheep are fast runners, and their specialized feet make them agile rock climbers. Bighorns have two toes covered by hooves that act like sharp toenails capable of snagging the smallest rock ledge. A soft, fleshy web between the toes and padding beneath the hooves provide grip and help the sheep balance on almost sheer rock faces. Hooves continually grow and are worn down by use.

Like all sheep, bighorns have a special stomach—one with four chambers, or sections—that allows them to eat coarse food such as dry grass and twigs. In the first chamber, called the rumen, bacteria and acids soften

the food. Then it is regurgitated, or brought back up
to the mouth. This food mass, called a cud, is chewed
again. When it is swallowed, the cud passes through all
four stomach chambers to be fully digested. Bighorns
graze on slopes and in valleys but never stray far from
mountainsides. Bighorns have keen eyesight and hearing
as well as an acute sense of smell. At the slightest danger,
a grazing bighorn will break for the nearest rock face and
cling to a tiny ledge, which predators such as mountain
lions, wolves, lynxes, bears, and coyotes will usually not
attempt to climb.

*Although young bighorns are
fearless in traversing rocky terrain,
overconfidence can sometimes
lead to disaster.*

Young bighorns must quickly learn about the surrounding area and how to evade predators in order to survive.

BATTERING RAMS

Bighorn sheep are social animals that live in groups called herds. Adult males typically gather in bachelor herds, while adult females and their offspring make up separate herds. A herd may contain 10 to 100 members. In summer, herds travel from place to place, grazing on mountainsides as high as 8,500 feet (2,591 m). Because the sheep cannot dig through deep snow to find food, herds move to valleys and forested areas below 3,000 feet (914 m) in winter. Here they find more tolerable temperatures, protection from snowstorms, and easier access to food. Mountain sheep are valuable in their **ecosystems**, because the foods they eat prevent overgrowth of vegetation. Sometimes a food source attracts sheep for other reasons. Ronald K. Siegel, a noted California scientist, discovered that mountain bighorn sheep often seek out a certain kind of lichen (*LY-ken*) that has a soothing **narcotic** effect on the sheep. The lichen grows on rocks, and the sheep scrape it off with their teeth.

A bighorn herd is based on **hierarchy**, with some sheep having more power than others. Bighorns

Bighorns can run up mountain slopes at 15 miles (24.1 km) per hour and across flat land at more than 30 miles (48.3 km) per hour.

Early snowfall can catch bighorns off guard, making it difficult to find food.

At 44 pounds (20 kg), 52 inches (132 cm) long, and 18 inches (45.7 cm) around, the biggest sheep horns on record belonged to a Rocky Mountain bighorn.

communicate their status in the herd largely through scent marking. **Glands** in a bighorn's face and feet secrete an oily substance that is rubbed on rocks and even on other sheep. Throughout the year, rams kick, nudge, and butt horns to establish ranking in the herd, but these fights are typically brief and rarely cause injury. In early October, however, the rams' behavior changes. In preparation for mating season, a period called rut, male herds break up into smaller groups away from each other. Group members aggressively kick and push each other, and they rub horns, comparing sizes. Two rams indicate a desire to fight by touching a nose to the other's hip and walking around in a tight circle—sometimes for up to an hour. Males under the age of seven typically walk away from such encounters, accepting their low rank in the herd. Only the strongest, biggest males in each group will compete for dominance.

At the beginning of a ram fight, two high-ranking males step away from the group and turn to face each other. They may paw at the ground and snort. Then, with their heads held high, they take several running steps forward. Just before impact, they raise their front

Rams may challenge each other to fight by rubbing eye secretions onto the bodies of would-be opponents.

Despite their instinct to fight, younger rams with smaller horns rarely win contests against older, bigger rams.

legs and drop their chins, crashing their horns together. Sometimes a third male will jump into the fight and bash one of the opponents before he has time to recover. After each clash, the males step back and turn their heads to the side, as if showing off their horns. A challenger will admit defeat by walking away to join the lower-ranking rams. Sometimes opponents will continue to fight on and off for several days. Each battle may last up to two hours, with grazing and resting periods in between. By the time the strongest males of each group have firmly established their dominance, all the fighting rams are exhausted and spend time grazing before moving into the female herds to mate. From late October into early November, as lower-ranking males linger on the fringes, dominant males remain in the middle of female herds, using their sense of smell to determine which females are ready to mate.

After a ram mates with one ewe, he will leave her and seek other partners. At the end of the rut, all the males return to their bachelor herds. After about a six-month **gestation**, a pregnant female will find a secluded place in which to give birth. Ewes typically have just one baby, called a lamb, per year, rarely giving birth to twins. A lamb is born with dark eyes and weighs between 8 and 10 pounds (3.6–4.5 kg). Its coat is woolly and grayish-white, and it has knobby horns. The newborn immediately begins feeding on the milk produced by its mother. Although a lamb is able to stand shortly after birth, its mother keeps it hidden for about a week so that it can learn her specific scent before it joins the herd. The first two weeks of a lamb's life are the most critical. Until it can learn to keep its footing on steep cliffs, it can fall. And because it cannot run fast, it will be vulnerable to predators.

At about three weeks of age, the lambs in a herd

Although lambs can eat grass within two weeks, it will not become their primary diet for several more months.

Unlike other sheep species, which often give birth to twins, bighorn twins are rare and have a lower survival rate.

form their own group, called a nursery herd, to spend their days playing and resting together. They go to their mothers only for meals throughout the day, relying on the nutrient-rich milk for their first five to six months of life. By the time the lambs are **weaned**, their coats have turned brown or dark gray and their eyes have lightened to a golden brown. When a lamb is 12 to 18 months old, it is called a yearling and may weigh as much as 100 pounds (45.4 kg). Female offspring remain in their mothers' herds for their entire lives. When they are about two years old, male offspring join bachelor herds.

Lambs learn from their elders how best to climb and leap around their rocky habitat. This agility helps bighorn sheep evade most predators, such as coyotes and cougars. When a bighorn sheep senses a predator's presence, it will bolt, signaling that the rest of the herd should run. However, this technique does not necessarily work on one predator: With a wingspan of greater than seven feet (2.1 m), golden eagles may swoop down on unsuspecting lambs and carry them away before their mothers even realize what is happening. Global **climate change** is another bighorn threat. Too much rain can cause flooding, while too little rain can stunt vegetation growth and decrease drinking water sources. Drastic environmental changes often affect young lambs and yearlings the most. If a bighorn sheep can survive its first year, it will typically live for 10 to 12 years. Some desert bighorn sheep have even been known to reach 17 years of age.

A larger cougar population in an area will drive bighorns to winter at higher elevations, where food is scarce.

Bighorn petroglyphs were carved into a Utah mountainside by San Rafael Fremont Indians between A.D. 600 and 1300.

The first humans to travel from Asia to North America likely did so by crossing the Bering **Land Bridge** about 12,000 years ago. They discovered herds of large animals such as bison, deer, and bighorn sheep, which became primary food sources. **Archaeologists** have uncovered evidence suggesting that deer and desert bighorn sheep were hunted as early as 2000 B.C. in what is now Arizona's Grand Canyon as well as in Utah and California. In these regions, ancestors of the Hopi, Zuni, and Paiute American Indian tribes covered cliff and cave walls with carvings and paintings called petroglyphs. Some of this prehistoric artwork features hunting scenes that include bighorn sheep. In addition, other cave sites in the same regions contained small twig figurines of such animals as deer and bighorn sheep. Split in half and probably soaked in water to make them bend, the twigs were bundled, shaped, and tightly wrapped into form. Some of the figurines even have tiny spears through their hearts. **Anthropologists** believe such figurines, called fetishes, were used in rituals intended to ensure a successful hunt.

Desert bighorn sheep eat cacti to get moisture and can go three to nine days without drinking water.

The wool of the merino, whose rams have curled horns similar to bighorns', is considered to be the finest wool of any sheep breed.

Near Phoenix, Arizona, more recent petroglyphs can be seen at South Mountain Park. Estimated to be between 600 and 1,000 years old, the rock art of mountain bighorns was made by a tribe—the Hohokam—who had disappeared by A.D. 1450. Later on, mountain bighorn sheep played an important role in Crow and Shoshone Indian cultures as well. Bighorns were hunted for their meat and skins, and their horns were used to make finely crafted bows that became valuable trade items. Both tribes appreciated the animal so much that they told stories that characterized bighorn sheep as noble, helpful creatures. One legend tells of a man who was possessed by an evil spirit and threw his son off a cliff. The pine trees reached out their branches to catch the boy, and the bighorn sheep took care of him. The sheep shared their powers of keen hearing, sure-footedness, strength, and wisdom with him. They named the boy Big Metal, and when he grew up, Big Metal returned to his tribe. The tribe then named the river that flowed through their land the Bighorn, after Big Metal's second family. Big Metal promised to use his skills to help his people become the best hunters in the land—as long as they never changed the river's name. In the 19th century, the Crow were commonly known as the best hunters in the region, and "Bighorn" was recorded as the river's official name in 1805 by French fur trader François-Antoine Larocque.

That same year, American explorers Meriwether Lewis and William Clark, traveling through the Bighorn River area, named the Bighorn Mountains. Other sites that are named for the majestic sheep of the region include Bighorn Lake, located in Montana's Bighorn Canyon National Recreation Area, and Bighorn Basin, a plateau that separates the Bighorn and Rocky Mountains in Wyoming. Branching off the Bighorn River, the Little Bighorn River flows through Wyoming and Montana. U.S. cavalry officer W. F. Reynolds, who led a number of expeditions in the West, named the waterway in 1859. In 1897, the U.S. government established Bighorn National Forest in northern Wyoming. It is one of the nation's oldest protected areas.

In the mid-16th century, Spanish explorers in what is now the Tule Desert of southwestern Arizona discovered hundreds of desert bighorn sheep horns stacked in pyramids. The remains of charred bighorn bones were

Visitors to Washington's Cape Disappointment State Park can view artifacts from Lewis and Clark's journey west.

VIRGINIA'S COUNTRY

A September afternoon in the Big Horn mountains! The air crystal clear; the sky cloudless; the outlines of the hills distinct! Elk Creek Valley lay golden in the sunshine, silent save for the incessant hum of locust and cricket, the hurrying of the creek waters, and the occasional bellowing of steers on the range beyond the foot-hills....

Moreover, on the barely visible brown road that threaded its way across the prairie, two specks were moving rapidly in the direction of the Gap. The specks took form, became two riders, a boy and a girl, on wildly galloping horses, which, neck to neck, tore at last through the Gap, forded the creek in a mad splash of water, stirrup-high, and dashed away up the Valley.

from The Girl from the Big Horn Country, *by Mary Ellen Chase (1887–1973)*

also found near the pyramids. Not until the early 20th century did scholars learn why such structures and bone piles existed. Descendants of the Pima Indians revealed that their ancestors believed bighorn sheep could influence the weather. The pyramids of horns were meant to slow the violent wind that blew across the desert, and the mounds of charred bones were used in a ritual intended to calm the spirits of the mighty bighorns, thus preventing fierce storms in the first place.

The bighorn sheep's reputation for strength and control has not diminished over the centuries. Today, bighorns symbolize durability in the form of Chrysler's Ram series of pickup trucks. First released by Dodge in 1981, Ram pickups featured Dodge's logo: the head of a bighorn ram with curled horns. Some models were outfitted with a hood ornament—a silver ram's head, which was first introduced by Dodge in 1933. Today's Ram pickups continue these traditions. Another tradition with a long history is Rams football. In 1937, the National Football League (NFL) adopted the Cleveland (Ohio) Rams, a team that took its name from the mascot of Fordham University and signified the strength and

For $1,400, American sculptor Avard Fairbanks was commissioned to create the first Dodge ram hood ornament.

In 2013, Russia released four stamps dedicated to native sheep and goats, including a bighorn cousin, the snow sheep.

The Rocky Mountain bighorn's scientific name, *Ovis canadensis canadensis*, means "sheep belonging to Canada."

agility of its players. The Cleveland Rams moved to Los Angeles, California, in 1946 and then to St. Louis, Missouri, in 1995. Throughout their history, the Rams have continued to reflect the reputation of their namesake by being fiercely competitive and tough.

As the state animal of Nevada, the desert bighorn sheep lends its name to the minor league basketball team the Reno Bighorns. Established in 2008, the Bighorns were affiliated with the National Basketball Association (NBA) Sacramento Kings as of 2014. At the college level, several teams besides Fordham have taken on the bighorn moniker. Colorado State University in Fort Collins and the University of Rhode Island in Kingston are among them.

From the Canadian Air Mail logo of the 1930s (featuring a ram standing in snow with an airplane flying overhead) to contemporary postage stamps, images of bighorn sheep emphasize males' impressive horns. A bighorn's face filled the frame of Canada's first bighorn postage stamp, which was issued in 1953. A 15-cent stamp released in 1970 depicted a group of bighorns on a mountainside, and in the 1990s, bighorn images were selected for special conservation fund stamps in British

Columbia and Alberta. In the U.S., the bighorn was part of a 1972 series of 4 endangered animal stamps, a 1981 set of 10 North American mammals, and a 1987 set of 50 animals from the 50 states. In 2007, a bighorn's face appeared on a 17-cent stamp. Far more valuable than postage stamps, gold and platinum collector coins featuring bighorn sheep were minted in Canada in 2014 and are valued at more than $3,000 each.

Among the hundreds of stone figures adorning Ontario's Parliament Hill in Ottawa are bighorn sheep.

In 1884, Dall sheep were named in honor of American naturalist William Healey Dall, known for exploring Alaska.

KINGS OF THE MOUNTAINS

bout 18 million years ago, the first sheep ancestors **evolved** in Asia, Africa, and Europe. These small, horned animals, called *Eotragus*, are commonly known as the dawn deer. Identified from fossilized horn cores found in North Africa, *Eotragus* evolved into a wide-ranging group of hoofed, grass-eating animals suited to a variety of environments. During one of Earth's ice ages, about 600,000 years ago, some of the earliest snow sheep crossed the Bering Land Bridge into North America. This animal flourished and spread throughout the mountainous western regions of the continent, evolving into the two distinct species of wild sheep we know today: Dall and bighorn. The Dall sheep remained in the cold northwest, and the bighorns moved south. Soon, bighorn sheep numbered in the millions and covered the entire western half of the continent from southern Canada to northern Mexico.

For thousands of years, **indigenous** peoples hunted bighorns for food and fur, but when European settlers began moving westward in the early 1800s, bighorns began to suffer. By 1900, careless overhunting left only a few

Since wolves returned to Yellowstone National Park in 1995, the bighorn sheep population has actually increased.

Bighorns' keen eyesight allows them to spot the movement of predators from up to one mile (1.6 km) away.

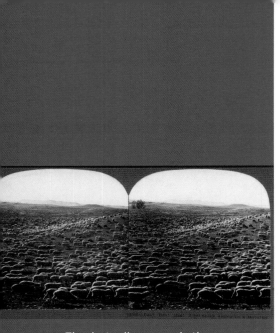

Thanks to disease and other threats, the large herds once common in the late 1800s gradually decreased.

In summer, bighorns eat clover, grass, and flowering plants such as lupines. In winter, they eat shrubs and small trees.

thousand bighorns in scattered populations throughout the West. In addition, from the 19th to the mid-20th century, bouts of sickness ravaged many bighorn herds. The introduction of domestic sheep, goats, and cattle into bighorn habitats resulted in the spread of diseases against which the wild sheep had no defense. Bighorns also suffered habitat loss and food shortages as human settlements grew and vast cattle herds took over grazing land.

In the 1930s, conservation efforts to save desert bighorns in Arizona were launched by several groups, including the Boy Scouts of America. The state established two protected areas in 1939 to help desert bighorns repopulate without human interference: the Kofa National Wildlife Refuge, west of Phoenix, and the Cabeza Prieta National Wildlife Refuge, near the Mexican border. In 1964, the Society for the Conservation of Bighorn Sheep (SCBS) was formed in California. Today, the SCBS works closely with the California Department of Fish and Wildlife and the federal Bureau of Land Management to assist in the protection and registration of bighorn sheep in California's deserts.

Land development as well as natural and human-influenced depletion of ground water has created serious challenges for California's bighorns. The SCBS operates a water monitoring and replenishment program that provides the animals with water. Several times a year, trucks haul thousands of gallons of water to special locations in bighorn habitat where tanks are kept filled. The tanks are connected to metal troughs from which bighorns—and many other wild animals—can drink. Electronic monitoring of the water levels automatically

An accurate count of desert bighorns in the Grand Canyon is difficult to achieve because of the area's rough terrain.

According to a 2007 U.S. Geological Survey report, as many as 2 million bighorns existed before the 1500s.

sends messages through a **satellite** communication system to alert the SCBS when the tanks need refilling.

Since the mid-1800s, bighorn sheep numbers have declined 90 percent. Colorado has the most bighorns—more than 7,000 in at least 75 different herds. While the mountain bighorn population is, overall, considered stable, scientists agree that herds containing fewer than 100 individuals are vulnerable. Because small herds are isolated from larger populations of bighorns, they lack genetic variability, which means that over time, the animals become too alike and less able to change to survive their environment—a weakness that could

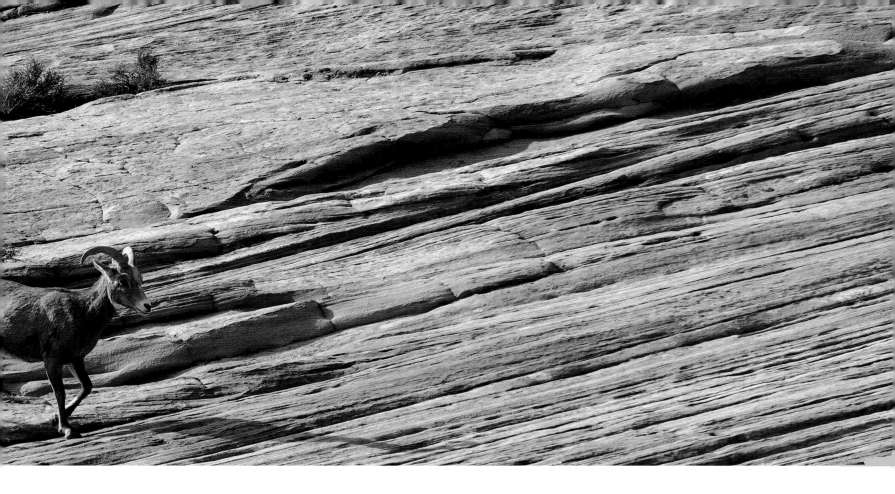

ultimately lead to extinction. In addition, domestic
sheep and goats continue to share bighorn grazing land,
and while domestic animals can be immunized against,
or treated to resist, many diseases, bighorns cannot.
Immunization keeps domestic livestock from getting sick,
but these animals may still pass on bacterial infections and
viruses. Scientists estimate that disease is the number-one
threat to desert and mountain bighorn populations.

Managing bighorns and keeping them healthy is a
challenge. In 2013, an outbreak of pneumonia caused
by the illegal dumping of dead domestic sheep killed
more than 100 bighorns in California's Mojave National

Radio collars do not interfere with a sheep's abilities to graze effectively or escape from predators.

Preserve. Wildlife biologists with the state's Department of Fish and Wildlife flew over the preserve in helicopters, dropping nets on bighorn sheep. Researchers on the ground tranquilized the sheep to make them fall asleep and then took samples of mucus from the captured bighorns' noses to test for the disease, which affects the respiratory system. Each sheep was then fitted with a **radio collar**. Such collars weigh about two pounds (0.9 kg), are made of several layers of heavy-duty belt material, and have an aluminum compartment for the battery—which can last up to two years—and a **Global Positioning System** (GPS) tracking device on the bottom. The GPS transmitter sends data on the sheep's movements to satellites, allowing researchers to learn how diseases such as pneumonia can be spread from one herd to another. The collars can be taken off recaptured sheep, but usually they are designed to simply fall off after a period of time.

Mountain bighorns are threatened by a strain of pneumonia carried by nonnative mountain goats that share bighorn habitats. The Greater Yellowstone Area Mountain Ungulate [hoofed animal] Project is a major

In 2012, Nevada Division of Wildlife biologists relocated 50 bighorns to southern Utah to help repopulate the area.

A helicopter brings bighorns to researchers so that they can examine the animals and fit them with tracking devices.

collaboration among the U.S. Forest Service, the National Park Service, and state agencies in Montana, Wyoming, and Idaho. Many people are involved in the capturing, testing, and tracking of bighorn sheep and mountain goats in a number of protected areas, including Yellowstone and Grand Teton national parks. Animals fitted with electronic collars that collect data on a microchip can be recaptured and the collars removed to retrieve the data. In addition, all sheep that are captured are subjected to **DNA** testing. A small blood sample is taken, and the information is collected in a database that gives researchers a picture of a herd's genetic variation.

Historically, human activities have influenced bighorn populations—for good and ill. For example, although bighorns are still hunted, fees paid by hunters fund most research and conservation programs. And although a certain number of permits are sold each year for bighorn hunting, the activity is allowed only in managed areas. The recovery of bighorns relies on many factors. As long as support for the revival of bighorn populations and respect for healthy and diverse ecosystems continue, bighorn sheep will live on as kings of the mountains.

Researchers at the San Diego Zoo study Peninsular bighorn sheep droppings to collect genetic data on the rare animals.

ANIMAL TALE: HOW THE BIGHORN GOT HIS CURLS

The bighorn sheep was respected by the native peoples who shared its land and was often featured in traditional pourquoi, or stories that explain how things came to be. The following tale is from the Kalispel (*kah-LEES-peh*) Indians of Montana and tells why mountain bighorn rams have tightly curled horns.

_____

In the old days, Coyote was a powerful spirit responsible for keeping peace among the animals. One day, he learned that Ram was driving animals over a cliff to their deaths. Coyote could not believe this and had to see for himself. He climbed to the mountaintop to find Ram.

"What are you doing up here?" Coyote asked.

"I am looking at the amazing beetles on the ground," Ram replied.

Coyote peered over the cliff to the grass thousands of feet below. "I don't see any beetles," he said.

"Look closer," Ram said.

Coyote leaned further. "I still don't see any beetles."

In those days, the mountain sheep had long, straight horns. Ram jabbed his horns into Coyote's back, pushing Coyote over the cliff. Coyote tumbled to the ground and landed amidst dozens of dead animals. His breath left him, and his world went dark.

After a while, Fox arrived and gave Coyote a nudge. Coyote opened his eyes. "I must have been asleep," he said.

"You were dead," Fox told Coyote. "Ram pushed you off the cliff."

"Strange," Coyote said. "I must find out why Ram is behaving so badly."

Coyote climbed back up the mountain and hid behind a tree to watch Ram. Presently, Blackbird landed in a nearby bush and began eating berries.

Ram called out to Blackbird, "Come see the beetles in the grass!"

Blackbird glided off the bush and hopped over to Ram. "Where?" he asked.

"Down there in the grass," Ram said, pointing. "Look!"

Blackbird leaned far over. "I don't see them," he said.

"Look closer," Ram said. And with that, he jabbed blackbird with his horns and sent the bird tumbling over the edge of the cliff.

Blackbird flapped his wings. "Are you crazy?" he called to Ram. "You could have killed me!" Then Blackbird flew away.

Suddenly, a deep voice boomed: "Foolish Ram. Don't waste your time with birds. Destroy the four-footed animals."

Coyote recognized the voice of the Evil One. He leaped from his hiding place and rushed to Ram. "You have been possessed by an evil spirit," he said, "but I will help you."

Coyote ran down the mountain and called out to the Great Spirit. "Ram has been possessed by the Evil One," he explained. "He is behaving very badly toward the other animals." The Great Spirit listened to Coyote with interest. "How can we save him?" Coyote asked.

The Great Spirit told Coyote what he must do. Coyote raced back to the mountain. "Come see the beetles in the grass," Ram said to Coyote.

"Forget it," Coyote said. And with that, he pushed Ram over the edge of the cliff. The Evil One, terrified of a painful fall, flew out of Ram's body. Coyote quickly grabbed Ram's long horns to pull him up. When Ram was safely back on the mountain, Coyote released his grip. Ram's horns snapped back so hard that they curled like ribbons. And they have remained that way to this day.

GLOSSARY

anthropologists – scientists who study the history of humankind

archaeologists – people who study human history by examining ancient peoples and their artifacts

climate change – the gradual increase in Earth's temperature that causes changes in the planet's atmosphere, environments, and long-term weather conditions

cultures – particular groups in a society that share behaviors and characteristics that are accepted as normal by that group

DNA – deoxyribonucleic acid; a substance found in every living thing that determines the species and individual characteristics of that thing

domesticated – tamed to be kept as a pet or used as a work animal

ecosystems – communities of organisms that live together in environments

evolved – gradually developed into a new form

extinction – the act or process of becoming extinct; coming to an end or dying out

gestation – the period of time it takes a baby to develop inside its mother's womb

glands – organs in a human or animal body that produce chemical substances used by other parts of the body

Global Positioning System – a system of satellites, computers, and other electronic devices that work together to determine the location of objects or living things that carry a trackable device

hierarchy – a system in which people, animals, or things are ranked in importance one above another

indigenous – originating in a particular region or country

land bridge – a piece of land connecting two landmasses that allowed people and animals to pass from one place to another

narcotic – a substance that affects mood or behavior

radio collar – a collar fitted with a small electronic device that sends signals to radio receivers

satellite – a mechanical device launched into space; it may be designed to travel around Earth or toward other planets or the sun

weaned – made the young of a mammal accept food other than nursing milk

SELECTED BIBLIOGRAPHY

Armstrong, David M. "Colorado Parks & Wildlife: Bighorn Sheep." http://cpw.state.co.us/learn/Pages/SpeciesProfiles.aspx.

———. *Rocky Mountain Mammals: A Handbook of Mammals of Rocky Mountain National Park and Vicinity*. 3rd ed. Boulder: University Press of Colorado, 2008.

Grassy, John. *Audubon Guide to the National Wildlife Refuges: Rocky Mountains*. New York: St. Martin's Griffin, 2000.

Hutto, Joe. *The Light in High Places: A Naturalist Looks at Wyoming Wilderness, Rocky Mountain Bighorn Sheep, Cowboys, and Other Rare Species*. New York: Skyhorse, 2009.

National Bighorn Sheep Center. "Wild Sheep Biology." http://www.bighorn.org/biology.html.

National Park Service. "Yellowstone: Bighorn Sheep." http://www.nps.gov/yell/naturescience/bighorn.htm.

Note: Every effort has been made to ensure that any websites listed above were active at the time of publication. However, because of the nature of the Internet, it is impossible to guarantee that these sites will remain active indefinitely or that their contents will not be altered.

Bighorns are an important link in the food chain, managing grasses and shrubs while providing food for large predators.